THE RITUALITES

THE RITUALITES

Michael Nardone

BOOK*HUG | 2018

The production of this book was made possible through the generous assistance of the Canada Council for the Arts and the Ontario Arts Council. Book*hug also acknowledges the support of the Government of Canada through the Canada Book Fund and the Government of Ontario through the Ontario Book Publishing Tax Credit and the Ontario Book Fund.

Book*hug acknowledges the land on which it operates. For thousands of years it has been the traditional land of the Huron-Wendat, the Seneca, and most recently, the Mississaugas of the Credit River. Today, this meeting place is still the home to many Indigenous people from across Turtle Island, and we are grateful to have the opportunity to work on this land.

Library and Archives Canada Cataloguing in Publication

Nardone, Michael, 1981–, author
    The Ritualites / Michael Nardone.

Poems. Issued in print and electronic formats.
ISBN 978-1-77166-455-4 (softcover)
ISBN 978-1-77166-456-1 (HTML)
ISBN 978-1-77166-457-8 (PDF)
ISBN 978-1-77166-458-5 (Kindle)

    I. Title.

PS8627.A735R58 2018   C811'.6   C2018-904272-9   C2018-904273-7

PRINTED IN CANADA

INTRODUCTION

Michael Nardone's poetry unsettles territories as it roves through the continent, documenting the neon signs and the billboards, the dinner table conversations, and the overheard terrors of everyday Americana. The book orchestrates unlikely and compelling movements between abstracted, parodic narrative and lyric elegy, which Nardone writes as modulated, cerebral laments for an era's failure to reach utopia. The poems map what we drive towards, driven mad, driving round the bends in form and through the American landscape—from Pennsylvania to South Dakota to Nevada. Witnessing geographic movement as a kind of living trespass, *The Ritualites* impressed upon me the need for re-tuning poetry's ethnographic ear, for transposing attention away from calcified "identity" and toward living, throbbing practices of civilian life across the United States.

Nardone's verses seem to take their cue from Muriel Rukeyser's citational, attentive documentation of the embodied devastations of corporatized and industrialized belts. In his parodic, aloof prose, the critical lathe seems poised to spin Lisa Robertson's claim in her succinct poem "Envoy": "analysis too is a style of affect." Episodic and variegated, the book's many voices are by turns ventriloquial and verisimilitudinous—sometimes welcoming a careful and attuned ear, sometimes shunning it; sometimes asking for sympathetic leaning, sometimes ironic distance. This is a book that wants the reader to be many-splendored and nimble. My hope has always been for poets to subscribe not to movements or schools of aesthetics, but to be the bearers of urgent form—form as a thing to be broken and held close, at once. Nardone's collection seems to carry that urgency, seems to know artifice for what it is—a holding pattern for thought's flight, so it can land in a stranger place, further, always, from the comforts of habit and home.

— Divya Victor

THE RITUALITES

Au revoir ici, n'importe où.

—Rimbaud, "Démocratie"

TOWER 1, TOWER 2

—O the pepper.—The pasta.—I hope we hear the one about California.
—Such a lovely song.—Such a lovely place.—The crushed pepper.
—At Grossman's my dentist I caught a commercial on his television
For that concert.—On the National Channel.—At 8.—Well you wait
Until the sauce starts to simmer.—It's nearly time.—Then add sugar.
—And your tooth Helen?—Had an ache.—But it don't hurt to eat?
—It does but Bob with all this good food how could I not help but eat?
—Sue this crab dip's sure delish.—Thank my Aunt Louise in California.
She sneaked the recipe from her fave Chinese buffet.—How much sugar
Should I use Sue?—Two tablespoons'll do. Then add a pinch of pepper.
—The pasta.—O Joe and that television!—Pass the pasta.—Wait wait
I can't hear one word what you're sayin.—The pasta.—The television!
Turn it down!—Say please.—Joe!—Why must he eat at that television?
—Please pass the pasta please.—Joe!—It's no use.—We'll have to wait
Till we have his attention.—Man I gotta say Sue! These stuffed peppers!
Fabulous!—I can't remember those words.—I just might have to eat
One more.—Words?—How it all begins. That song. About California.
—Fab. Plain fab.—Save space for cake Bob.—Gotta watch my sugar.
—Cake!—O no.—No?—O no.—Something bout an alibi.—Your sugar?
—Means his diabetes.—So no dessert for me.—That goddarn television!
—Sue you three should see Louise.—Bring me the crushed red pepper.
—Maybe take her to Disney.—O they got it all. Eat in Italy. China. Eat
In Mexico. Wherever.—Member Disney Jay? We took him to California.
To Disneyland.—You member Jay?—No I don't remember.—Wait wait.
—You just go from one to the other.—O.—Morocco.—No.—Tokyo.—Wait.
O let me think.—Really is a small world after all.—It wasn't California.
It was the World. Florida! O that place! Like walkin inside a television!
—Coffee? Tea?—Coffee.—Coffee!—Tea.—Coffee.—Coffee.—Cream? Sugar?
—A dreamworld. A cartoon.—Both please.—Looks like Joe could eat
Some more.—Coffee Joe?—He's deaf as can be Betty.—The pepper.
—O will you take this to your grandpa. He don't eat without that pepper.
—I can hear it in my head.—Dessert's on!—And turn down the TV.
—A dark desert highway.—Here we go.—Sue that's too much sugar.
—Eat your cake Ange.—Cool wind in my hair.—Stop singing and eat.
—What on earth is that song?—It's 8 everybody.—O I really can't wait.
—But why that bit about colitis in the air?—That's the Motel California!

—I do hope they kill that beast.—And his uniform!—My god more rain.
—Did you see his uniform?—To me it seems it's all inside their head.
—I mean what is this thing they sing of?—You know. Those inner voices.
—Same one he wore on the Enola Gay!—Inner voices? What a lot of talk!
—Woulda been one hell of a parade.—We should do some kinda toast.
You know it's not every day we're all here together.—Less and less I fear.
—We do this each week.—See what I believe the song's about is the fear
Of endless pleasure.—You gotta shut that window Bob. Before the rain
Comes floods the kitchen.—That's right Jay. Someone oughta do a toast.
—But it's like the night man says. We are programmed to receive.—Talk
About nonsense.—I always thought it's about what drugs do to your head.
—Could be our new tradition.—Uncle Hal did drugs and he heard voices.
—Was his conscience dear.—For years Bob's been hearin the voices.
Germans. Always talkin in his ear whisperin like.—Yes sometimes I fear
My mind still moves in and out of the war.—Mein Bob. Mein.—We talk
About it sometimes.—Hello the window.—Quick just look at all the rain!
—Hello there!—Hello?—Anybody listening?—I said we'd do a toast.
—Something.—Who's gonna do it?—Anything.—Gotta be Jay the head
Of the table.—Bob you okay?—Jay!—Bob do you hear us?—In my head
I always hear the ocean.—Bob?—Jay!—Think he's hearin those voices?
—Still don't believe they canceled the parade.—If no one won't I'll toast
Myself.—To us!—Postpone it maybe but.—But?—These are times I fear
We've forgotten about our soldiers.—Cancelled? Because of a little rain?
—Those men are heroes.—Boom!—Survivors.—Betty please I can't talk
About it anymore.—A blast from the past!—God Bob.—How can you talk
Like that.—Summer soldiers all of them. A touch of rain and they head
For the hills.—Rhine Bob. Rhine.—Rhine?—Rain Bob.—Like the rain
In Spain falls mainly on the plain.—Now here she goes with them voices.
—O leavin on a jet plane.—Don't know if I'll be back again.—Well I fear
For the worst.—Now there's somethin to toast.—Toast? I don't want toast.
—Can't hear a thing can he?—Nope.—No Joe. Not toast. Toast! Toast!
—To us!—What?—Nothing!—To us!—He can't hear us over all the talk.
—Sure comin down.—That line about the prisoners stuck in my head.
—Prisoners?—Of our own device.—Stop with the prisoners. Bob's voices
Will start up again.—Shakes'em good.—The window!—Bob nothin to fear
Sittin here havin ourself a meal.—Nope nothin really.—Only a little rain.

O, OR, PLAINS, PENNSYLVANIA

Away from a relative plane of table conversation,
    The last forks and spoons resume a familiar
Progression, clattering the sink's tin basin in time
    With Aunt Ange's O! no! oblivion. Laugh tracks
Wrangle down the hall, jingles clump, APPLAUSE
    Lights up — cues an interlude of who's on sale —
Have it your way right away be all you can be just
    Do it. Soon it's static. So the drowsed
Shuffle off to a continent of sleep; they will retire
    There, trim some hedges, craft umbrellas, maintain
A permanent muzak. Like that, a pulse of snores
    Crowds the house, then shush, they scatter once
The windows inhale — through, over the tree peaks —
    Out, aimless away, over Susquehanna.

Over Susquehanna, rising through piled culm
    Mountains, a once-upon-pastoral tamed
By strip-mall persuasions, banks, chrome-candied
    Gas stations, abandoned sedans, vans, fast
Eats, neon billboards flashing tomorrow's lottery
    Winnings — $6.2 MILLION — Claim Your Fortune
Today, additional parking, burbs crumbling
    To kindling, a school bus slumped, wheels
Sunk in a roadside sludge moat, windshield shards
    Gravel-split, telephone poles tipped, spilt milk
Cartons, tossed socks, hubcaps, cans, plastic sacks,
    A whitetail laid low across the highway.
Now birch trees disperse for guardsman and gate
    Both bearing the crest of Woodbridge Estate.

The stately post-teen gatekeep with a full fat lip
    Of tobacco dip is the one we call Red Head Ron,
Short, somehow, for Reginald—self-proclaimed
    Hater of Homos, who once pressed his combat
Knife against my neck so he might inquire, O
    How's it feel to stick that prick into a fire-
Bush? (Meaning L, famed since age thirteen.)
    Does she sport a red-eye like mine? This
As he pitched that blade to spread his ass across
    O's face: standard procedure, perhaps, to prepare
For our Armed Forces, where Ron will one day
    Campaign across endless red deserts fulfilling
His birthright to fight like his father, a Vietnam
    Veteran, town's quick-for-a-script allergist.

The kids with dibs on their parents' prescriptions
    Work fast to crack them, crush them, line
Them right up, sniff and knuckle their nostrils.
    Blank ghosties keen on upcoming fixes
Breeze by, lithe in thick flocks, aflight. We watch
    One stagger, stop, search an edge, then belly
Flop. Agnes May, our host and entertainer, flaps
    Top half ashore the crumbled concrete pool—
More leaves than water—lipstick smeared chin to
    Ear, smashed martini glass mapped into her
Palm: Love, a chaser, quick! she spouts, then slips
    Back. Body at our feet, toe-deep in the shallow
End, together, crouched, when at last we roll
    Her over, a voice sighs among us: O mother.

The woman's her mother, says one flashlight cop
        To another. Guess we'll take your old lady
Any place that admits her—the General, Saint Jude's
        Or the Geezer. Cap'n Notepad asks her name:
Lilah. Lilah May. Some questions for you, Lilah May.
        You live here? Indeed. Age? Sweet sixteen. Why
The crowd? We're celebrating our right to assemble.
        Been drinkin? Iced tea. How bout your mother?
Who knows? I can't attend every swallow. No doubt
        With dinner she sipped her chardonnay. We know
Agnes well. Mom's a sociable creature, loves a man
        With a badge. Yeah she told us that much
When we tugged her Benz from the creek bed. Sir,
        I don't aid her ways nor repeat them.

Scenes repeat beneath each word and speak into
    A lapse. And time, unhinged from its sediments,
Rifts against the seeming, shapes the only sense
    That makes: crystal bits of chandelier stud the red
Shag rug, through rooms in a row where inundation
    Tales get told, black tar passed, shades tae kwon do
All over the peeled-key piano while Lilah strips
    The walls back to cinder. And Agnes stalks home,
Arm around Ron—O those eyes I know!—yawns
    Her head in half. Strike a match once the power
Outs, palm it face to face. Who knows, no, how
    Far, you, one from another, slip? There, you's
Fixed? Bottle in A's bandaged hand raised to clink
    A glass. There, when the last light flits.

Firefly-lit, the field pulses. Our footfall,
   Dissolved in the tall grass, in midsummer's
Swelling hum, stalls on the brink. Blackbirds
   In a blue mass rise. And sure that O would chase
Her, trace her stride into the thick brush, and
   Lost there, touch her knotted fabric on a low
Branch, and as that branch snaps, hear her
   Dash back into a clearing, a moment's path
Expands in the green blink, as the face, her hands,
   Our body—slips to the ground, her knee to
My lips—O takes hold of her waist and, inching
   Down, tastes the moist blades stuck to her bare
Calves, when L stops, stands, spins her back
   To the wind, unfurls a blanket.

Whimpies! Pigs in a blanket! Corn? Real Indian maize!
    A thumb sucked for the final gob of mayonnaise.
In lawn chairs gathered round, everyone conducts,
    Hands dubbing their stomachs, a choir of digestion.
Holy man, Ange, that frangipane flan was all the rage.
    To die for! Fab. Plain fab. Bottle rockets fizz
Above the backyard fence. Grey kidneys of cloud
    Sag down. A nervous tic, how Grandma picks each
Bit-O-Bacon glazed on the picnic table and feeds it
    To her teeth? Sweet relief, some lemonade
The horseflies haven't colonized. We must not fear,
    States the radio. Those skies will clear. Think
Positive, people. Here's the tune that's sparked a new
    Dance craze that's bound to sweep the nation:

Variation: soaks down dandelion, marigold
        Punctures, spreads. Rises, bursts. Blends. Again
The blond lobs against the glare. Again the.
        Again the firecracker timpani. Everything
In fits. Flares fleshed to the pole star fade. A wind
        Change. Inflection: left perspectives right,
Holds, gold and silver fold, fold. Everything fits.
        And did the feeling? Did it was it true
For you? O say you see it too. Sure the dead
        Don't undress and swim in their bleeding. Cracks
Red, red and blue. What should be the Old Glory
        Blows away while forming. Send me down
Where the winds roll over. Burnt white, a wind
        Comes avalanche. Smoke screens the atmosphere.

Smoke bombs fog the parking lot. Flung from above,
    A dud hisses at my shoe. Scuds of Southern
Comfort, spat right back, scorch our legions' clash.
    IROCs rev, Def Leppard blasts. As some crawl
Back down the river path, a horde of thumbs advances
    Clicking remote control keys. Locks unlock,
Alarms whirl off. A silhouette pleads Christ! Every
    Exit bottle-necked, a jeep jumps the curb,
Thumps a bollard, swerves to a stop. Red Head
    Ron drops from a lamp pole, squats, sucks back
His spit: The Red Coats are coming! Up-chuckling—
    Huzzah!—his guts across the blacktop, he
Slips, yet insists it's his turn to drive, as he boots
    The passenger side wide open.

Open fusebox, expired sparklers. Spaghetti strands
    Slither out a can. Dovetailed etcetera up the steps.
Tripped; balcony rail scissor-tips; insulation hail.
    Soypools. Hornets gangbanging eggrolls. Bunk
Bed Stonehenge, sand. Top News at Ten: I'm just mad
    About Saffron. Saffron's mad about. Inconceivable,
Says National Channel. My name is Inigo Montoya.
    You killed my father. Prepare to. GLAD® Bags
ForceFlex® diamond stretch design prevents rips even
    When overstuff. They call me. Grand Marshal
Deak Parsons chats with parade-goers as they wait out the.
    100% Polyethylene. Electrical banana's gonna be.
Agnes? My name is. Is that? As you wish as you wish.
    The blast still echoes in the silence of this room.

The blast still echoes in the silence of this room.
   You undo you don't you no listen once you
Run. Through fields you how could you do? Mute
   You mute you. Kick the doors down burn
The furniture bursts the air. To the driveway drag
   You brittle limbs you forehead hole your tooth
Marks the gravel. Go. No be okay now go you
   Know you must you know. When then the head
Lights someone has come. But if they follow if
   If you don't. Wait here go this won't. Should it
Would that way where could we go? On the verge of
   No this won't. Wait here go I won't. Wait here
Yes this won't. I told L to wait there did you
   Wait here did you wait there or did you run?

O, of where, sun from what? Blurred blue red, O
   Be some other name. Treeless, leaves lift. Streams
The wind streams the wind streaming wind. Through,
   A route persists. Shall I speak at this? Again,
I've slipped within the glimpse, again what proof
   Still holds, still flits, while these hopes dissolve
Into compulsions that uplift?

                              Shall I speak at this?
   The matters of faction, once dismissed, begin
And end an elemental shift. Morning swarms down
   From the forehead of the mountain; shadows sift
Below with gossiped prophecies of home, welcoming
   O unto a relative plane of table conversation.

TO WHOMEVER FINDS THIS NOTE

A tiny kitten sits next to me. Watching.
A dog barks. The birds gather on the
telephone wires. Let all the story of this
People Temple be told. Let all the books be
opened.

UNFIXED TERRITORIES

Consider the alternative state in which you now reside.

Take a big deep breath.

It's no accident you are holding this book.

Every event we experience and every person we meet has been put in our path for a reason.

This is a social world, and you are a social animal.

So don't just *read* this book.

Interact with it!

Underline your favorite passages!

Make this book *your* book.

Try writing your own thoughts in the margins.

Personalize it!

We were in the early years of a long struggle.

Our way of life, our very freedom, had come under attack.

Who did this?

I looked at the faces of the children in front of me.

I heard people yelling my name.

For months I had been praying that God would show me how to better reflect His will.

As you read this book, try to stand apart from your self.

You are not your feelings.

You are not your thoughts.

As you read this, notice what information you receive, and by notice I mean: *simply observe.*

You deserve to feel great about your life.

Try to project your consciousness into the corner of this room and see yourself, there, in your mind's eye, reading this book.

Can you see yourself almost as though you were someone else?

I looked out on an abandoned, locked-down Washington.

The moon and the stars and the planets had all fallen onto me.

We were standing in the middle of a whirlwind.

Who am I, that I should go to Pharoah and bring the Israelites out of Egypt?

There's only one person in the world like you.

You are the totality of the universe acting through a human nervous system.

Everything you did before this moment has no reality.

You hear the voices of a clamoring chorus inside your head.

It happens in a context called the world.

Inner life depends on thousands of signals coming into it.

Adopting children through the mail can be an extremely positive experience.

You must keep your focus on the *here* and *now*.

Only what you are doing in this moment, only this, is real.

You must help You.

Life *is* a competition. They *are* keeping score. There *is* a time clock.

Give up your goals.

Think of your life as the game board of this book.

You can relax now.

You are in a glorious moment filled with possibility.

I had a philosophy I wanted to advance.

I thought of the lyrics from one of my favorite hymns, "God of Grace and God of Glory": "Grant us wisdom, grant us courage, for the facing of this hour."

I took a look at the list of techniques.

Was I willing to forgo my anonymity forever?

I fought back tears.

I christened our plane *Great Expectations*.

There would be time later to mourn.

If you want to be a pilot, you must control the machine and not let it control you.

A few minutes later I felt the plane bank hard to the west.

I hugged the flight attendants and assured them that everything would be okay.

AIRPORT NOVEL

The airframe shuddered as high-velocity metal thwacked through its structure.

Staring at the full-length mirror, Joe hardly recognized himself. He wore a Western shirt with snaps instead of buttons, tucked into a pair of skintight jeans. His belt had beadwork all around and a huge brass buckle with the graven image of a bucking horse. The boots were tight enough to cramp his toes, and he felt awkward in elevated heels.

"That's it." His partner grinned. "They love the rough stuff."

They had rifles after him in a moment. The spattering of the revolver shots had given him a moment of hope, for the way the mustang was dodging among big rocks, he had a reasonable guess that they might keep on missing their target. But when they opened up with rifles, he knew the trouble was on him.

The kitchen was clean to a gleam. Maybe that's what women did, or some women, when they were coping with grief. They got out cleanser and a mop.

"Perhaps the human mind can deal with only one intense experience at a time."
"And poetry is, of course, an intense experience."
"One of the most there is."
She smiled at him, her face lit up with the intimacy of a shared confidence.

"It's coming back up!"

Her lips parted under him, but he didn't rush in. Instead he took her lower lip between his and sucked once before releasing it. When he did it again, she reciprocated with his top lip. He stifled a groan.

"We have confronted America."
"Isn't this highly dangerous?" one of their number asked.
"In the short term, yes."

A stunned silence in the big office followed these words. Stern was shaken, Hemple on the point of collapse. Tica stared at Hector, white-faced, overwhelmed by the change from the taciturn, quiet man she had faced with confidence when she began her trip to this planet.

She fiddled lengthily with some papers, eyes down.

The man from Justice said: "The President has reviewed your case, and he feels that you have served enough time. He believes that you have more to offer your country and your community by once again becoming a productive citizen."

Pilot and copilot relaxed, the aircraft on autopilot and all the gauges within norms.

"It's—it's strange. You know I'm not American, don't you?"
"No, I didn't know that or anything else."
"My family—I supose you would call them gypsies," she said, faltering.
"Then how—"

As his words echoed above the tumult, Rachel felt an eerie up-welling in the water beneath her. Like a massive locomotive straining to reverse direction, the slab of ice had groaned to a stop underwater and was now beginning its ascent directly beneath them. Fathoms below, a sickening low-frequency rumble resonated upward through the water as the gigantic submerged sheet began scraping its way back up the face of the glacier.

"This is karma. This is everything I've done, coming back to take a big bite of my ass."

His motivation was partially personal. His own fortune had suffered badly in the events of the previous Friday, drawn down by hundreds of millions. The nature of the event and the way his money was spread around various institutions had guaranteed a huge loss since he'd been vulnerable to every variety of programmed trading system. But this wasn't about money.

The explosion was immediate and catastrophic. It blew the tail and both engines off the airframe. The main fuel lines, which ran just under the deck, were vented to the sky, and the fuel that was being pumped created a meteor-like trail in the sky.

"Oh, Lord," Viveca whispered. Everyone turned to follow her gaze. Consuelo had materialized in front of the mariachi band. She was dressed in a leopard-print jumpsuit, even though the invitations had asked for white clothes only. She was singing along with the mariachis, beating time with a cocktail glass in her hand.

"Goddamn it," former President of the United States John Patrick Ryan muttered into his morning coffee.
"What is it now, Jack?" Cathy asked, though fully aware of what "it" was.

He walked over to the picture window in the living room and couldn't help noticing his reflection in the mirrored wall. The light from the setting sun cast amber highlights on his gleaming skin, brown shadows heightened the muscularity of his lower belly.

"A quagmire, as we all know now—"
"To people who dislike military operations, there's always a quagmire to jump into."

Panting, he collapsed on the nearest divan.

Langdon's thoughts began to spiral—dreams, memories, hopes, fears, revelations—whirling above him in the rotunda dome. As his eyes began to close again, he found himself staring at three words written in Latin: *E pluribus unum.*

"Out of many, one," he whispered, again nodding out of consciousness.

"Timmy..."

"Will you wait a minute?" he said, annoyed. "I'm trying to find your ice cream."

"Timmy...something's here."

He hurried out of the freezer and heard a low hissing sound, like a snake, that rose and fell softly. It was hardly audible. It might even be the wind, but he somehow knew it wasn't.

"Timmy," she whispered. "I'm scared."

He crept forward to the kitchen door and looked out. In the darkened dining room, he saw the orderly green rectangular pattern of the tabletops. And moving smoothly among them, silent as a ghost except for the hiss of its breath, was a velociraptor.

The gorillas did not care why human beings were there, or what reasons had brought them to the Congo. They were not killing for food, or defense, or protection of their young. They were killing because they were trained to kill.

Edmunds's breathing was coming in ragged gasps over the intercom. "Can't see very well—I feel—jellyfish—hurts—so many—my arms—burning—hurts—they're eating through—"

"Jane, come back. Jane? Are you reading? Jane."

"She's fallen down," Harry said. "Look, you can see her lying—"

"We have to save her," Ted said, jumping to his feet.

"Nobody move," Barnes said.

"But she's—"

"Nobody else is going out there, mister."

In the broad and infinitely complicated world of nature there is a certain dependence of one form of life upon another, much like a giant tapestry woven from myriad threads into a complex pattern: each thread by itself means nothing and is very delicate, but in the warp and woof of the design each is immeasurably strong and meaningful.

Zahara marched to the fax to retrieve the incoming message.

"The machines should be destroyed. Every last one of them, and all their parts. The pretense that by building a machine rather than by purifying their hearts humans could stand at the right hand of God must be expunged, root and branch, before it is too late."

Phones rang in the secret Virginia headquarters of the cybercrime squad.
Chicago: "What the hell is going on?"
Los Angeles: "Can you fix it? Are *we* next?"
Detroit: "Who is behind these actions?"

Behind them, Sam cleared his throat, then went to stand looking out the window as the sun set.

"Ellie, can we really be sure that this isn't a message from—"
"From God?"
"Or from the Devil?"

TOPOLOGIES/OTOGRAPHIES

Well hello O

Pebble for your thoughts

Hey come on let's interlocute

Havin a bad day

Hatched from a black egg

O you make me laugh

I can always count on you for that

There was a row O

Didn't ya know

My ears both burst

Everything's been cancelled

I want to be clear O

Cleared

I'm atom's ant

Amamus a mass

I mean it I do

An adamant man

If you go I won't

This place could play home

I'll talk with the breeze

I'll sleep in a horse

No matter to me O

You and your swivelling eyes

[Centralia]

Let's hunt O

Let's see what we find

What first

I mean which way

When I think of everything I've eaten

I'd eat it all right up again

My cape for a Hong Kong Buffet

We'll eat wind O stones

Scavenge what's left of this city

Fresh soot more snow

Nothing in the bins but tinfoil

I'd bite your bones

If I could I won't

Hold on what's that

A juicebox some scraps

Quick O pounce

Sink your teeth in the gristle

A swell time O sublime

We should keep this Thursday's thing

You know where I'll be

Good of you to come out O

I do know

Nature loves to hide

[Centralia]

Terracotta tunnel sludge moth

Glass birch sun cinder chalk

Dustgirter coresample toothsplatter hoof

Camerado shimmer panopticon sleeve

Stroller coupon bangarang bulb

Muffin tourniquet vaseline tongs

Seizure flop insulin fit

Scaffold cuffs scanners hanger ducts

Profitbaton forklift ting

Sinkhole lull sturgeon curds

Hummingbird syrah

Tigerbeat marzipan placenta socket

Skittles crocuses antifreeze

Lungmonger thrust document

Icon customer gunt patrol

Dearthdads slaughterjuice jaws

Bazooka tang esophagi stack

Tusk stammer chunky surrogate throb

Crumble butter oxen flocks

Naugahyde whipits dogbody flaunt

Toons muppets aqueducts

Abudhabis serengetis pigsblood fleas

Writs wrists rope cement

Horses gulls dusk chimneys snow

[Far Rockaway]

And buffalo herds

Swift pronghorn

Winnebagoes lined

As far as the eye can see

Concrete tipi

Barbwire tumbleweed

Lewis & Clark

In cardboard cutout

PLACE YOUR HEAD HERE

Bluecoats

Do a ghost dance

My children my children

Name in stone

Name in stone

Your gangrened knee

Your radiant beard

Winter winter spring spring

Horsemeat horsemeat

The guns of the dead the gold

In them hills

Horsemeat the manna

The name in stone

UNKNOWN

Here comes their calvary

[Needles Highway Overlook]

Wherefore my glorious

Template unseen

Sent before discount etymolygies

Rid there of custom

Commentary not confounded

Chloroform refers with alertness

Behold my perjury hands

Command essential domestic activity

Scattered by the price of liberty

Judgement seat our legacy fends

Faults of man reign days bask

Inundated with the concrete spasm

Resolutely twanged

Grab him by their handle

Fury cluck interpretation thereof

With what gift I admit

The time is arrived our ear is appointed

If they say earth move

Earth makes move mountains

Rise up and fall

Upon that city it is written

[Provo]

Hindus Pray to Goddess Meladi to Fix Economic Crisis Global Warming
Workers Riot at Chinese Toy Factory Massacre in Mumbai 100 Dead
Madonna Leaves Her Guy 420 Tons of Tainted Milk Destroyed in China
Wal Mart Guard Trampled to Death 2 Dead in Toys R Us Shooting
No Way to Stop Us Says Pirate Leader Kidman Loses It on Letterman
Palin Back on Campaign Trail Bush to Pardon Bald Eagle Killer
Clinton Named to Obama Cabinet Bombings Tear Through Baghdad Mosul
NATO Trucks Attacked in Pakistan Protestors Beseige Bangkok Airports
What Next for Moshe Holtzberg Venice Floods Knits a Rugged Comfort
HIV Doubles in Europe Cruise Ship Escapes Pirates Congress Slams Treasury
Bush: Unprepared for War Sorry for Economy 250,000 Jobs Lost November
Culture War to Erupt This Christmas Productivity Slows Wage Pressure Up
China Shuns West's Finance Sector Rwanda Linked to Congo's War
Too Fat to Fight Afghanistan Returns to Destitution Mugabe Must Go
Evictions in Hebron Rape in East Congo New Plan for EU Unity
Canada Suspends Parliament Is Lonesome George Infertile
Prostitutes Also Feel Crisis UK Troops to Leave Iraq Zimbabwe Bleeds
Blackwater Guards Charged in Iraq Killings Riots Shut Down Greece
US Border to Be Watched By Drones Cancer Overtakes Heart Disease
Somber Eid in India US Forces Mistakenly Kill 7 Afghans
Massacre in Congo Despite Support 48 Killed in Iraq Restaurant Attack
Dems Urge Blagojevich to Quit F-18 Crash in San Diego 3 Dead
Northeast Ice-Ravaged 800,000 Lose Power Last Visit to Iraq for Bush
Bad Times Draw Bigger Crowds to Church Jellyfish Overtake Tourist Resort

[Times Square]

48

Charity

Your black dress babe

Put it on

And get that bod back to the bar

Whaddya mean

Quit fingering your remote

Danny gonna get ya

Chocolate sauce martinis

To soak inside that throat

Babe

Don't straight your hair

Nah I know

There is salt in the air

Whaddya want me to do

The oceans full of it

Ourite ourite

Time to go so hangin up hun

Click

[The Chicken Box, Nantucket]

Am kiddin

Come on

Get over here

Everyones waitin for ya

Me and Dan

And there's a band

Playin Stairway to Heffin

Knew that'd getcha

Seeya on the patio

Bye babe

Wooh

Time for this girl to sink or swim

And belief me

The chick don't swim

Yeah dear

Two beers here

You can put that on my tab

Therese

[The Chicken Box, Nantucket]

Ladies and Congressmen

The publicity stunt

We've all been waiting for

I am ready

To negotiate wait

I refuse

To do details

Simmer down now

Data exists

To support this

My business

It's not intelligence

This absence is

Evident I demand

No outcome someone

Tell me when

Is the humanitarian

Airdropped

[Cactus Springs]

Whaddaya say Gills

How's your knees

Shock and awe cakewalk huh

Manifest your custody

I have wept

With your widow

God bless our troops god

Bless America boy

They stinks right

Up to them teeth jeez

We gotta keep this optimistic

It just might be our last

Night ever man

Beings and fish can coexist

It's simple see

This steadfast progress

We'll abandon

Market principles

Save

The free world

[Fort Sumter]

AIRPORT NOVEL

"It appears we're in some sort of cave. I wonder how big it is."

South of the Coronado Bridge, the muggy air began to congeal. American industry and Mexican charcoal fires turned the sky into sludge.

"Did you bring the money?" the man asked, his voice tight with an anxiety that strummed the air. He wore dress slacks an inch too long, hems pooling around scuffed department-store loafers. His old leather jacket was done up against the bitter March night, but misbuttoned.

"Did you bring the money?" he shouted again as he glanced around the park.

The bathroom door swung open. Jaime Rivas—blow-dried and splendid in an Italian suit and loafers without socks—strolled out of the darkened room, zipping up like he'd just finished filling the urinal. In his left hand he carried a silver-plated semiautomatic pistol.

"Citizenship is just a piece of paper. The roots of your soul are another thing that can never be cancelled. Never."

Slowly, the words in the books began to resonate with something deep inside her, began to take on meanings that went beyond the words themselves. She couldn't quite put her finger on exactly what it was, maybe something like a current she could ride, a door she could step through, or both. But there was *something* — and it called to her. So what at first she had been doing out of desperation she began doing willingly, and then even eagerly, though she hid that from her captors.

"We have lost a material war — but spiritually we shall never be vanquished."

He looked out over the beach and felt the hot wind like the breath of the Devil. Heard the flutter of canvas. Smelled the tang of wood smoke. With that smell another beach floated up in memory. Far away, and long ago. But he'd never forgotten. Who could forget a place like Vietnam?

The wind blew harder and a flash of lightning lit the swollen clouds waiting on the horizon.

"Jesus shit Christ," Jason said to himself. "God," he said aloud. "Goddamn it." His teeth ground against one another.

He finished his microwave pizza and then cleaned his plate. He pulled on his pants and found a clean blue shirt in his closet. He turned on the taps to wash his face and found the usual trickle of lukewarm brown water. He clipped on his badge, grabbed his thick winter coat, laced up his boots. As he walked out the door, he felt almost relieved. What would be would be.

The golf cart rolled to a stop at the far end of the facility. Overhead two birds swooped and cawed, making lazy circles around the perimeter of the high slanting roof.

"Now what should we do? Should we keep going and see where this will take us?"

He speculated a little as he rode through the faultless gray softness of predawn.

Was history doomed to repeat itself?

Not used to such carnal images invading his thoughts, he stood up, agitated, and strode across the room, poured himself another shot, swallowing it back in one gulp. There was no doubt about it, he must try working with them as a team.

"May God put the right words into our mouths now."

UNFIXED TERRITORIES

You are about to set out on the most transformative adventure of your life.

Let's begin this exercise by emptying your bladder and, if possible, your bowels.

Mastering the art of connection hinges on a willingness to go deeper with others, to be intimate.

Inhale and relax.

Mastering the art of connection requires a vulnerable act of expression, of sharing your innermost being with another.

All that Nature asks of you is to listen.

Be me.

This requires some new thinking.

Take two deep breaths.

Really assume that you *are* me.

You feel like me.

You are where I am located right now.

Lie on your back with your knees bent and feet in the air.

Stick out your tongue and curl it lengthways to form a sort of tube.

Take two or three quick inward sniffs.

Turn over on your stomach with your legs apart, and your arms up above your head as though you are swimming the butterfly stroke.

Breathe.

Our destination is not a place, but a way of looking at things.

Now allow your body to go completely limp.

Imagine losing your keys and looking all over the house to find them.

This is not a theory. This is life.

Somewhere thousands of miles from where you are sitting, a leaf is falling from a tree.

This is the mind at work.

You are thinking about what is on my mind.

Being loved feels good.

You know what I want to do, and you know what I have done.

If someone throws a ball at you, you don't have to catch it.

Every feeling you are having is my feeling.

When you have a thought — any thought — that's all it is: a thought!

You are me.

You identify with labels. You feel a need to conform.

You are asleep at the wheel. You can't sleep. You wake up in a panic.

Your motto is: "Not always right, but never in doubt."

You are totally closed to any opportunity for learning information that may contradict your strongly held and poorly founded beliefs.

You are proud of it.

You have a little man inside your head who keeps talking and talking.

You are not your body.

You are not your body.

You impose an extreme and unrealistic standard on yourself and others.

You have trouble with words.

You use guilt to control and manipulate others.

Do not let this be some dry rhetoric in a book.

I am speaking directly to you.

You sold out your dreams.

You said the words.

You got in the backseat that night.

You blew up.

You expected to be put down or rejected.

You bought it.

You got married.

You ate it.

You chose these feelings.

You quit.

You need to let go of the grip you have on your own body.

Imagine yourself inside a hollow chamber with no top and no bottom.

There you go.

Exhale through your mouth while uttering a long vowel sound of your choice: for example the "e" in "we" or the "o" in "go." Let the sound last the length of the exhalation.

You are rising to a new level of being in which presence matters for itself alone.

How free we are when we dream!

Let this thought amplify and contain your solitude.

You are lighter than a breeze.

Choose from a variety of villas on the beachfront, in gardens, or on stilts over the lagoon.

Wake to the sound of the crashing waves and open the doors to your private deck and feel the gentle sea breezes while you order breakfast from your personal butler.

Lose yourself in holistic massage therapies, total relaxation techniques and as much Chinese tea as you want.

Sail to the Temple of Poseidon.

Take a micro flight over the desert or enjoy a 4x4 safari.

Order a picnic and visit Angkor Wat.

Discover the exotic Shona sculptures of Zimbabwe.

Notice how the intense light that inspired so many artists highlights the rich pure colors of the natural landscape.

Dolphin watch at the Gulf of Oman.

Unwind with a unique selection of rum-based cocktails while soaking in the warm sunset and spectacular view of the iridescent South China Sea.

Prepare yourself for a day filled with activities, from scuba diving, fishing and sailing to yoga, tennis, water aerobics or a shopping trip to a nearby traditional village.

Enjoy a coffee in a café overlooking the Grand Canal.

Find a shady spot in the tropical gardens and relax surrounded by lily-filled ponds, banana palms and exotic flowers.

Take time out for a leisurely ferry cruise along the Bosphorus.

Discover more about the life of the Mongolian nomads who build sturdy round tents and tend their horses, sheep, and camels.

Indulge in a revitalizing herb and spice body wrap.

In the evening, sip cocktails while watching a scintillating African sunset.

In the early morning, go on a game drive to see elephant, lion and giraffe, or take a balloon safari over the plains.

Venture to the spot where Aphrodite is said to have risen from the sea.

Try your hand at mini golf.

Take a helicopter ride over the spectacular coastline to the sugar cane plantation for a private tour of their famous rum distillery.

Go diving among magnificent reefs with green moray eels, lobsters, pretty coral formations and a vivid array of brightly colored reef fish.

Watch the comings and goings of yachts.

Wander down the path from your villa past clumps of flowering hibiscus and bougainvillea towards a gleaming white sandy beach set under the deepest blue cloudless sky.

Enjoy an endless supply of refreshing drinks served by attentive and friendly staff.

Swim in the hot springs of a nearby volcano.

Return in the evening to enjoy freshly grilled seafood accompanied by gentle Brazilian music.

Spend the day lazing on your villa terrace, gazing at nothing but the ocean as far as the eye can see.

AIRPORT NOVEL

The scream was high-pitched and continuous.

An infinitesimal second passed, and the very foundations of the city imploded in a blaze of crimson and silver.

"I love you," he mouthed to Tina as he hugged their kids and the evening sun angled across her hair and made it glow.

"I know," she said, resting a hand in his hair and stroking his head. "I think I was beginning to figure that out."

Through human mouthpieces, the bosses communicated their expectations. There would be no end-of-the-world parties, no doomsday loss of decorum. There would be no orgies, no mass suicides.

"Man evolves through suffering. As light requires the dark to realize illumination, so divine Law decrees that good should be tempered by evil. God is Absolute, eternal truth beyond all vicissitudes of mortal men, but mystics suspect that God, though perfect, needs deeper perfection, so is dreaming into existence an endless sequence of universes, each conditioned by the character of its predecessor that He might learn vicariously from the experience of all creatures, humans, spirits, on all planets in all the planes of His Creation."

"Who is this? Who is this *hideous* and *foul* man?" Helen gasped.

As the sirens faded, the world grew quiet.

"This is Caper One to Vandal Deca. Over."

Comroe picked up the microphone. "Reading you. What's going on?"

Shawn, his voice tight, said, "Sir, we see bodies. Lots of them. They appear to be dead."

"Are you certain, Caper One?"

"For Christ's sake," Shawn said. "Of course we're certain."

The cars were, for the most part, orderly. They sat quietly, idling and leaking exhaust. They were lined up all along the highway as if at any moment the trouble ahead might clear and the traffic would surge forward. Brake lines shone red. Hazards blinked. The cars seemed alive. Their occupants were not.

"What happened?" Barbara asked. She showed John her phone. "I can't get anyone..."
"Everyone is gone," he said. He kept rolling the three words like a mantra over and over in his head. "Everyone."

Gunfire crackled east of them. Sometimes the rounds were from soldiers, sometimes from random rage. Looters were certain to come that night.
"You have a gun?" he said.
The earnestness in his voice made her anxious. "Of course."
"What kind?"
"A .38?" She tried to not say it like a question.

Beyond a crossroads they began to come upon the possessions of travelers abandoned years ago. Boxes and bags. Everything melted and black. Old plastic suitcases curled shapeless in heat. Here and there the imprints of things wrested out of the tar by scavengers. A mile on and they began to come upon the dead. Figures half mired in the blacktop, clutching themselves, mouths howling.

"The world is a goddamned evil place. The strong prey on the weak, the rich on the poor. I've given up hope that there is a God that will save us all. How am I supposed to believe that there's a heaven and a hell when all I see now is hell?"

With the first grey light he rose and left the boy sleeping and walked out to the road and squatted and studied the country to the south. Barren, silent, godless. He thought the month was October, but he wasn't sure. He hadn't kept a calendar for years. They were moving south. There'd be no suriviving another winter here.

"It's over," Fowler said.
Tolby nodded. "I know."
Silvia hesitated. "Do you think—"
"Think what?"
"Did we make a mistake?
Tolby grinned wearily. "Hell of a time to think about that."

The tears that had been burning inside her eyes and throat all day broke free. She wanted to scream, to tear at her hair, to beg God or the universe or anything for a way to change her fate.

The president's hands trembled as he set the dossier down on the table. "And those remaining? Rounded up and put in camps for ... for what? For twenty years?"

"Sir, it's necessary," Philips told him. "If we don't do it, this will be the end of the human race."

Shut your eyes, dear reader. Do you hear the thundering of wheels? Those are the train cars rolling on and on. Every minute of the day. Every day of the year. And you can hear the water gurgling—those are prisoners' barges moving on and on. They are arresting someone all the time, cramming him in somewhere, moving him about. And what is that hum you hear? The overcrowed cells of the transit prisons. And that cry? The complaints of those who have been plundered, raped, beaten to within an inch of their lives.

In the police van, Jason sat hunched over, smoking and meditating. "Don't give up," the Jesus-freak officer crammed beside him said in the darkness.

"Why not?" Jason said.

"The forced-labour camps aren't that bad. During Basic Orientation they took us through one; there are showers, and beds with mattresses, and recreation such as volleyball, and arts and hobbies; you know— crafts, like making candles. By hand. And your family can send you packages and once a month they or your friend can visit you." He added, "And you get to worship at the church of your choice."

THE RITUALITES

We live on an island

I mean I don't know *all* the history

It's never really understood

Where is home

The landscape drifts

This is my climate

And now we've all arrived

And the doors are locked

So there's the street and all its people

We were talking about coincidence last time we were here

Now here we are

A coincidence

We have this quesion

Whether or not there are still experimental places

With everything becoming a gallery

Officially and actually

Bureaucratically

I think that's what people miss

These spaces of transitional happening

Where there are all these peaks and folds

A different sense of time

I go back trying to find moments that were real

Moments not forming some solid meaning

But in relation to relation

You too are a part of that trade

It's a kind of magnetism

Try and render it readable

You reach this new velocity

Hello

I know you

I mean

I know I know you

I know what you mean I mean

I know what you meant

This *isn't* real life

We're all on the record

That's why everything I've said so far is completely made up

Should we sit here

Can we sit here

There aren't enough seats

It's nothing sentimental

Come on in and give up your autonomy

I afford you

I have the capacity to bear your investment

But what should we do with the interest

Where's the door

How about we all stop talking and start groping one another

Picking and choosing eclectically

It will be a conceptual work

Everyone will feel obliged to pick up the reference points

No

This is the opposite of what I intended

Yes

Lo and behold they mesh

Perhaps this zone has its own time only your wrist receives

The sheer number of dead birds is unusual

I don't remember what we were doing

Something about the history of human beings

How do you spell your name

I remember I remember

There's the Zen practice of writing on water

Which is a collapsing of the French words for *death* and *mirror*

Am I wrong

Am I wrong

I miss my daughter

Six months ago you wouldn't even recognize me

It's good I've made decisions

It's not a private act

Theses things have their convulsive moments

Your mind goes out your ear

Once again

It bursts into dispersion

Once again

You materialize the mutter

No and yes

We've been over this a thousand times

The ocean is bottomless

Space is endless

The hour is a clock

It seems necessary to make these connections

A noise begins to swell

Their names are in the air

Across the sky

The clouds enlarge

We owe each other everything

I haven't been talking much

But I've got stories

Behold my nervous system

Do I still get to court you

It's something we're all taking part in

Living is going to be this wonderful cocktail party

All these small disagreements

The way they explode

A big bunch of shapes and sounds

This is actually happening

And sure enough

There is this moment

I can not help you

Thank you

Thank you so much

Lovely to see you

It was truly something

Take care

I always expect it to happen like that

Love is something that happens in Iceland

How should I transcribe the laughter

I am not going to speak about his clavicle

What's left is our will

The answer is yes

How do I reply to such a question

Am I supposed to reply

LA PUSH

If ever

There is if ever

There is
Ever there

If ever
There

     is other
Other

     than
Where it was
If

    ever this
If ever there is
No more
No other than

       if

Ever this

Other if ever there

Is other

Other than

Where

      it

Was if ever there

Is—

ENVOI

And with the taste of all

Our talk, a staircase

To where? They never knew, or

Never wished to. Still, they moved

On and by and through

Whichever way they could, came right

Close to you.

If only *we* knew

How the nights whirled by

In a phosphorescent thrum, tin cans

Strung from bumpers, how

The days unmeshed

Once shed of such sustained

Reticence, they might have been

A home. Yet all that's left is

Ocotillo, ocotillo . . .

A tune that makes your tonguescape

Dessicate. Even the cacti

Have shrivelled into little cattle

Skulls, as our morning

After's antimatter drones beneath each

Word.

Has it come to this, now that our love

Schlepped its act back north

To shack up with a sack of bricks? O

Lordy, no, we never

Laughed SO much, this you write, now

Cauliflowers are sprouting out

Our eyes — What bliss! Again, I slip

Within the glimpse, off into the selfsame

Disquietude your limbs

Refuse. I won't remember you

Each time Great Slave

Breaks up. Just being here is almost

Enough —

       "No,

This won't — That's all

Spruce smoke." Your scent. A music

Loses its

Furniture. Full stop. No more

Songs collaged with dooby doos, no ditty — *If*

The stars won't shine / If the moon

Won't rise — to hum

Your way home. We're through with this

Or it's through

With us. Things change

Their name

In order to keep

Quiet.

There is an opening in the earth

Recovered by the sky. It exists

So to speak within

Its disappearance. You and I

Can find each other

There whenever we want to, should we

Want to, even if

Less and less we want to. Where your body stops, there

The air begins. A decade of winds

Won't reveal us.

The beachfront's neo-conquistador lushness

Is

Soundtracked with bad jazz. Waverunners

Glide into the sunset. A real *coup*

De grace with a glass cock and cup o'

Coke creams

Their nose, the tip of which

Dips into the real

Thing, babe, while I backfloat

Dune to dune, tuned to a frigatebird's drift.

They're PTERODACTYLS—

We are sure of this. And then the blue

Flowers! The blue flowers! Above the mountains!

Tell me what they say!

Hey hey hey,

My my.

      I mean, what

Good is it to construct a code to conjugate

The Unknown? Someone

Always comes to math this up and add

It to the files: Antiquated Ideas; Bungling; False

Concepts; Confusion. Think

Of a perfect circle! Silos implode.

The called-up past

Collapses. Each insignia, its signature

Fade.

      And we go on—the days unregulated, this withness

Brought forth

From what latitude?

        "I will meet you there."

Among the terminal halls, invariously, they stroll

Without particular destination. Duty Free?

They enter, relieved

To find fellow Americans. "Hors?

Taxes?" "What

Kind of country is this?" Such dissonance

Anticipates our meltdown. They flaunt an inability to choose.

Meanwhile, exchange remains firmly

In their favor. In Basra,

For instance, they afford grain

Silos, astrolabes, dine on apricots and dream

Of Hammurabi; at Bala Hissar,

They sleep with ease, vacationers to the vacated.

Their anthems interchangeable—HELL

IS REAL—ELECT REGGIE RUST—MY MOMMY CHOSE

ABORTION—CONSOLIDATE YOUR LOANS—

BIRTH INJURY? IRREVERSIBLE ILLNESS?—EVERYTHING

MUST GO—Slogans

For a pitched-up swarm, and yet

You lend your ear

Automatically, suddenly, sometimes irreversibly.

This is transport.

                When the hydrants

Burst, then the sidewalks sway.

                        Bye-Bye Versailles!

Sayonara Toodaloo! Nothing to do

Except inspect this apparatus we're threaded

Through, and hold close

Amid the recomposed lines that divide

The serrated countryside. "In the future, flames

Will possess the still of objects

Stolen from the past," an ever-widening

Presence attests.

O

Particles aggregating into density, density bursting into

Motion, dispersing into ether as a wave —

A sound

That swims out

As the surface swims over —

NOTES + SOURCES

The composition of *The Ritualites* utilized a number of sound recording and transcription processes. Thank you to the family, friends, and various interlocutors who have contributed their words and phrases.

"Tower 1, Tower 2" is dedicated to, and in memory of, Robert L. Davis, Betty Davis, Joseph Nardone, Helen Nardone, and Angela Chico.

"To Whomever Finds This Note" is an excerpt from an anonymous letter — sometimes attributed to Richard Tropp — found near the airport runway at Jonestown, Guyana, in November 1978.

An initial version of the "Unfixed Territories" and "Airport Novel" series was dictated at the Edmonton International Airport while detained by the Canada Border Services Agency on 4 February 2011. The poems draw on the literature available at the location: paperback bestsellers, self-help books, security pamphlets, and travel brochures. Although no complete list of the sources encountered there exists, three books were central to the poem's composition: *The Sum of All Fears* by Tom Clancy, *The Self Matters Companion: Helping You Create Your Life from the Inside Out* by Dr. Phil McGraw, and *Decision Points* by George W. Bush.

"Topologies/Otographies" is part of an ongoing series of site-specific recordings, the location of which is documented at the bottom of each poem. "La Push" is also a part of this series.

"The Ritualites" is a transcription of phrases from an ambient recording made in Victoria, British Columbia — at a studio near Open Space — to mark the occasion of a reading and dialogue with Lisa Robertson.

"Envoi" is assembled from recordings and transcripts composed in Guaymas, Yellowknife, Montreal, and Pointe-aux-Chênes. A few phrases in the poem originate in books encountered at these locations: Kristin Ross's *The Emergence of Social Space*, Ryszard Kapuscinski's *Another Day of Life*, Joan Didion's *Play It as It Lays*, Phil A. Neel's *Hinterland*, as well as the song "You and Me," by Penny & The Quarters.

ACKNOWLEDGEMENTS

Excerpts from *The Ritualites* have appeared, often in different iterations, in *Lemon Hound*, *Poetry is Dead*, *The Coming Envelope*, *Oxford Poetry*, *Event*, *Le Merle*, *Matrix*, *Hobo Magazine*, *Canadian Literature*, *Cordite Poetry Review*, and *The Enpipe Line*.

In 2012, JackPine Press published an excerpt from the book, composed in collaboration with the artist Jude Griebel, as a limited-edition scroll entitled *O. Cyrus & the Bardo*. In 2015, Gauss PDF published an excerpt from the work as a chapbook edition entitled *Airport Novel*.

To Divya Victor, thank you for your insights and rich commentary while editing this book.

To Helen Guri, Collen Fulton, Corina Copp, Tim Lilburn, Erin Robinsong, Aisha Sasha John, Nicole Raziya Fong, Shiv Kotecha, Diana Hamilton, Cecily Nicholson, Pablo Alvarez-Mesa, Ada Smailbegovic, Lisa Robertson, Charles Bernstein, Jonathan Sterne, Jordan Scott, Donato Mancini, Anastasia Piliavsky, Erin Freeland Ballantyne, Pablo Saravanja, Jay MillAr, Hazel Millar, Kevin Lo, Mark Johnson, Don McKay, Mary Dalton, Lorna Crozier, Kristina Keitel, Seth Merrill, Alex Shisler, and Craig Chisholm — your thoughts have informed this work throughout its writing. Thank you.

Endless love and gratitude to Uma Freeland Nardone and Heather Davis. This book would not be here without you both.

ABOUT THE AUTHOR

Michael Nardone is the author of *The Ritualites* and *Transaction Record*. He is a postdoctoral fellow in the département des littératures de langue française at the Université de Montréal, and an affiliated faculty member at the Centre for Expanded Poetics, Concordia University. Born in Pennsylvania, Nardone has lived and worked in Boston, Varanasi, Berlin, and Yellowknife. His writings, dialogues, and editorial projects have been published widely and are archived at soundobject.net.

COLOPHON

Manufactured as the first edition of *The Ritualites* in the fall of 2018 by Book*hug.

Distributed in Canada by the Literary Press Group: lpg.ca

Distributed in the US by Small Press Distribution: spdbooks.org

Shop online at bookthug.ca

BOOK
PRODUCTION
WAR ECONOMY
STANDARD

Edited for the press by Divya Victor
Copy edited by Avril McMeekin
Type + design by Kevin Yuen Kit Lo, LOKI